EXPERIMENTS WITH MOTION

A TRUE BOOK®

by

Salvatore Tocci

Children's Press®
A Division of Scholastic Inc.

New York Toronto London Auckland Sydney
Mexico City New Delhi Hong Kong
Danbury, Connecticut

This photo is
full of motion.

Reading Consultant
Susan Virgilio

Science Consultant
Robert Gardner

The photo on the cover shows
a tennis ball in motion.
The photo on the title page shows
a spinning top.

Library of Congress Cataloging-in-Publication Data

Tocci, Salvatore.
    Experiments with motion / Salvatore Tocci.
    p. cm. – (A true book)
    Summary: Projects and experiments explore motion and the forces
that cause motion, covering such topics as inertia and resistance.
    Includes bibliographical references and index.
    ISBN 0-516-22603-7 (lib. bdg.)   0-516-27467-8 (pbk.)
    1. Motion—Experiments—Juvenile literature. {1. Motion—
Experiments. 2. Force and energy—Experiments. 3. Experiments.} I. Title.
II. Series.
QC133.5 .T64 2003
531'.11—dc21

                                                    2002001593

Contents

What's Your Favorite Movie?   5

Why Does Something Move?   9
   Experiment 1: Dropping In
   Experiment 2: Staying in Place
   Experiment 3: Forcing It to Move
   Experiment 4: Stopping Its Motion

What Kinds of Motion Are There?   23
   Experiment 5: Swinging and Spinning
   Experiment 6: Tilting From Side to Side

What Can a Moving Object Do?   30
   Experiment 7: Making Sounds
   Experiment 8: Lifting It Up

Fun With Motion   39
   Experiment 9: Speeding Along

To Find Out More   44

Important Words   46

Index   47

Meet the Author   48

A movie is a series of pictures that are projected on a screen so rapidly that you think there is motion.

What's Your Favorite Movie?

Do you know why a movie is also called a motion picture? A movie is simply a series of pictures that are projected on a screen. The pictures are projected so rapidly that you think objects on the screen are in **motion**, or moving.

The history of motion pictures goes back to the 1870s, when two men made a bet. One of the men believed that there were times when a race horse in motion had all four legs off the ground. To win the bet, the man arranged for a photographer to take pictures of horses as they raced around a track. The only cameras available at that time, however, were too slow to take the pictures needed to settle the bet.

A race horse in motion can have all four legs off the ground at the same time.

It took the photographer more than ten years to come up with a way to take pictures of race horses in motion.

The pictures showed that there are times when a race horse does have all four legs off the ground. The photographer became so interested in motion that he started taking pictures of other animals in motion. He even developed a device to project these pictures onto a screen. These were the first motion pictures. People used these pictures to study the motion of animals. All you have to do to study motion is carry out the experiments in this book.

Why Does Something Move?

Saying that something is in motion is another way of saying that it is moving. Some things are easy to get moving. Others are hard to get moving. Still others are almost impossible to get moving. No matter how easy or hard they are to get moving, all these objects have something in common. They all have **inertia**.

Inertia simply means that an object at rest is not going to move unless you do something to it, like push or pull it. This idea was first proposed by an English scientist named Isaac Newton in 1687. His idea became known as Newton's first law of motion. Part of Newton's first law states that an object at rest tends to

Which would you rather get moving— the football or the football player?

remain at rest because of inertia. But do all objects have the same inertia?

Experiment 7

Dropping In

You will need:
- tall jar with wide mouth
- table
- scissors
- cardboard
- quarter
- pencil
- paper

Set the jar on the table. Cut a square piece of cardboard a little larger than the mouth of the jar. Place the cardboard over the mouth of the jar. Set the quarter on the cardboard so that it is over the mouth of the jar. Use your finger to flick the cardboard square off the jar quickly. What happens to the quarter?

Place the cardboard on the jar again. Trace the outline of the quarter on the paper. Cut out the circle. This time, set the paper circle on

12

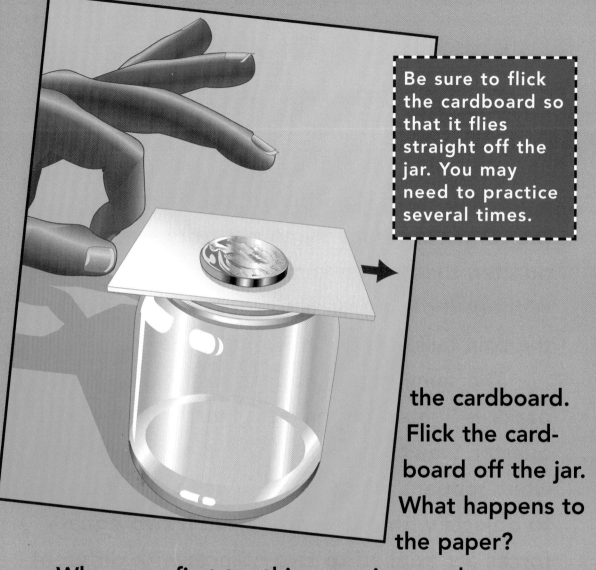

Be sure to flick the cardboard so that it flies straight off the jar. You may need to practice several times.

the cardboard. Flick the card-board off the jar. What happens to the paper?

When you first try this experiment, the quarter and paper probably will fly off the jar and land on the table or the floor. But with practice, you should get both of them to fall straight down into the jar. You should have less trouble getting the quarter to do this than the paper. Because the quarter is heavier, it has more inertia than the paper does and is harder to move. So when the cardboard goes flying out from under the quarter, the quarter remains where it is. Without the cardboard to support the quarter, the coin falls straight down into the jar.

The same thing happens to the paper. The paper is lighter and has less inertia than the quarter. Newton's second law of motion states what happens when equal forces are applied to objects with different inertia. If two equal forces are applied to two objects with different inertia, the object with less inertia will move more easily.

The paper has less inertia than the quarter and is therefore more likely to move when you strike the cardboard with the same force. As a result, the paper does not fall straight down into the jar as often as the quarter does.

Experiment with other objects to test their inertia. You can use a button, a piece of candy, a metal washer, or a ring. Are solid objects the only things that have inertia?

Test each object ten times. The one that falls into the jar the most times has the most inertia. Can you rank the objects, starting with the one that has the most inertia?

Staying in Place

You will need:
- measuring cup
- water
- cooking oil
- table
- food coloring

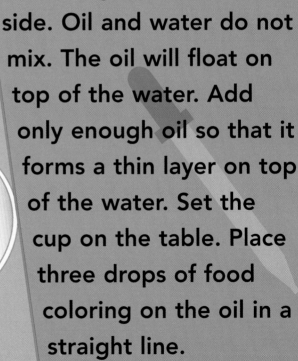

Fill the measuring cup halfway with water. Tilt the cup and carefully pour the cooking oil down the side. Oil and water do not mix. The oil will float on top of the water. Add only enough oil so that it forms a thin layer on top of the water. Set the cup on the table. Place three drops of food coloring on the oil in a straight line.

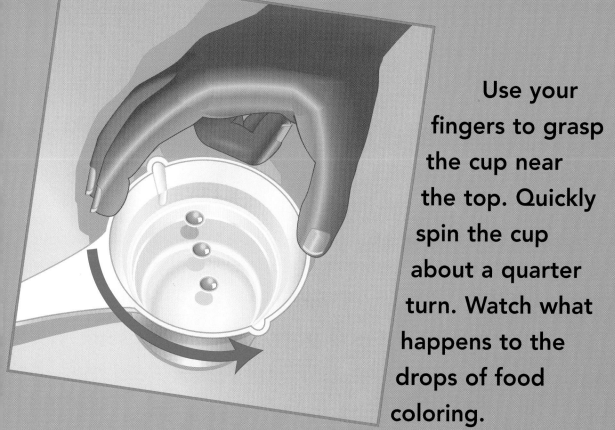

Use your fingers to grasp the cup near the top. Quickly spin the cup about a quarter turn. Watch what happens to the drops of food coloring.

Like solids, liquids have inertia. Because of their inertia, the water, oil, and food coloring do not move even though you spin the cup. It's hard to tell whether the water and oil did not move. But it's easy to follow the drops of food coloring. They stay right where you put them because of inertia. If everything has inertia, then why does anything move?

Experiment 3

Forcing It to Move

You will need:
- empty plastic bottle with narrow neck
- tissue paper
- paper cup
- measuring tape
- transparent tape
- quarter

Remove the top from the bottle. Wet the tissue paper with water. Fold the paper to make a plug that fits tightly into the neck of the bottle. Place the paper cup upside-down over the bottle. Aim the bottle away from your face. Use both hands to squeeze the bottle quickly. Watch what happens to the paper cup. Measure how far the cup moves through the air.

Repeat this experiment, but this time tape the quarter to the bottom of the paper cup. How far does the cup travel this time?

When you squeeze the bottle, you force the air out of it. As the air rushes out of the bottle, it pops the paper plug. The plug then pushes the cup into the air. The force of the air rushing out of the bottle starts the

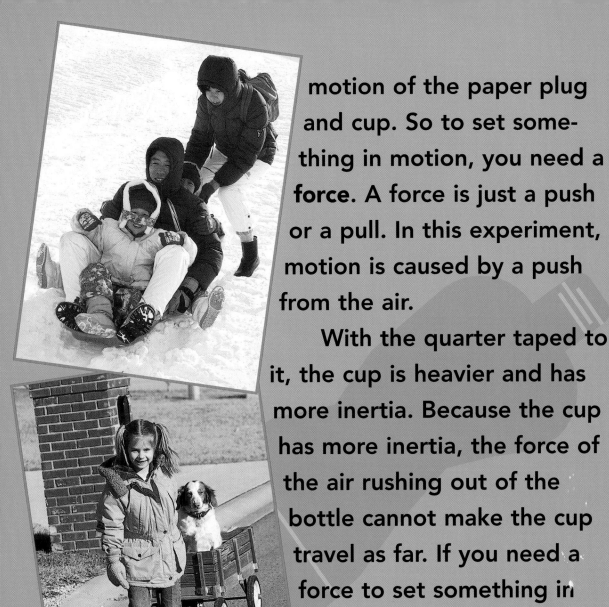

motion of the paper plug and cup. So to set something in motion, you need a **force**. A force is just a push or a pull. In this experiment, motion is caused by a push from the air.

With the quarter taped to it, the cup is heavier and has more inertia. Because the cup has more inertia, the force of the air rushing out of the bottle cannot make the cup travel as far. If you need a force to set something in motion, then how do you stop its motion?

You need a force to get the sled and wagon moving.

Experiment 4

Stopping Its Motion

You will need:
- hard-boiled egg
- large bowl
- raw egg

Place the hard-boiled egg in the bowl. Spin the egg. Grasp the egg gently with your fingers to stop its spinning. Then quickly let go of the egg. What happens? Do the same with the raw egg. Does it do the same thing as the hard-boiled egg?

The push you give both eggs overcomes their inertia and starts their motion. In the case of the hard-boiled egg, both the shell and the egg inside are solids. When you grasp the egg, you force both solids to stop their motion. So you also need a force to stop an object's motion.

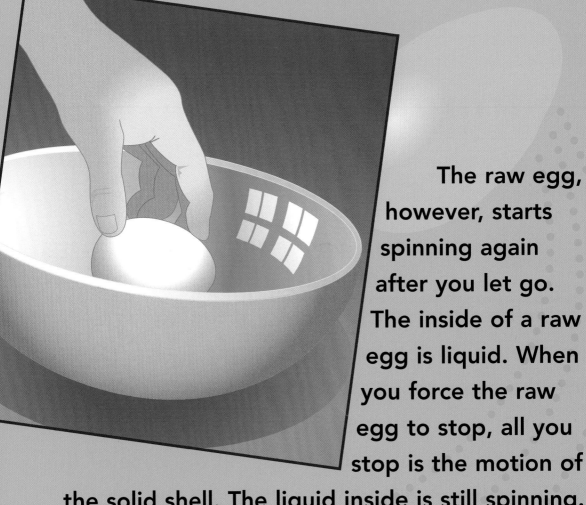

The raw egg, however, starts spinning again after you let go. The inside of a raw egg is liquid. When you force the raw egg to stop, all you stop is the motion of the solid shell. The liquid inside is still spinning. The spinning liquid provides the force that makes the raw egg start spinning again after you let go of it.

What Kinds of Motion Are There?

You can see many kinds of motion at a football game. A player running for a touchdown is showing forward motion. A quarterback dropping back to pass the ball is showing backward motion. A football flying through the air is showing spiral motion. There are many other

kinds of motion. For example, one kind of motion occurs when an object swings back and forth. Another kind of motion occurs when an object keeps moving in a circle. Here's a chance to learn something about both these kinds of motion.

Swinging and Spinning

You will need:
- dried peas
- small plastic bucket with handle

Place a handful of dried peas into the bucket. Lift the bucket by its handle and begin swinging it back and forth. Slowly make the bucket swing higher and higher. Keep swinging the bucket so that it starts spinning around in a circle. Do any of the peas spill out of the spinning bucket?

A force keeps the bucket and the peas in motion, spinning around in a circle. This force also keeps the peas from spilling out

25

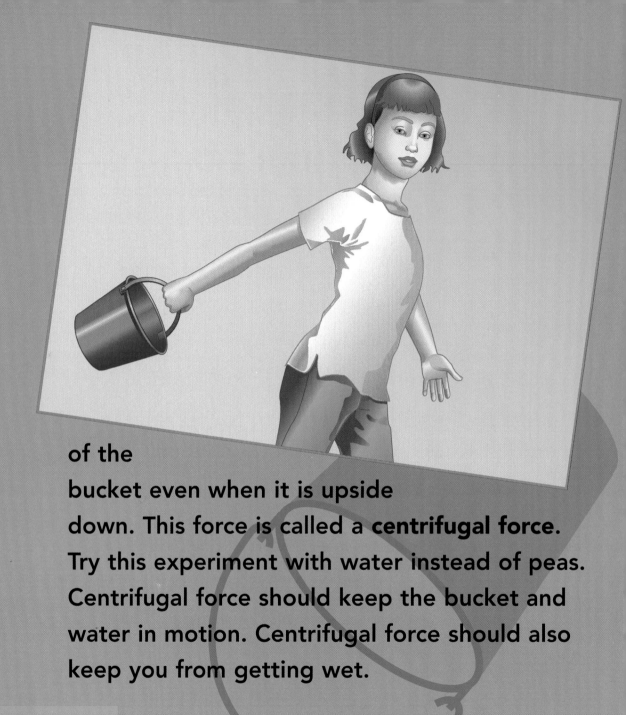

of the
bucket even when it is upside
down. This force is called a **centrifugal force**.
Try this experiment with water instead of peas.
Centrifugal force should keep the bucket and
water in motion. Centrifugal force should also
keep you from getting wet.

Tilting From Side to Side

You will need:
- ruler
- pencil
- cardboard
- scissors
- string
- LP record

Use the ruler to draw a square with 3-inch (8 centimeter) sides on the cardboard. Cut out the square. Use the pencil to poke a small hole in the middle of the cardboard. Tie a knot in one end of the string. Thread

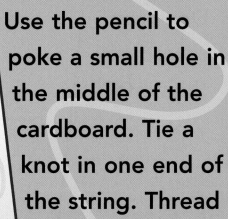

If you cannot get an LP record, try using a large circle cut out of a glossy piece of cardboard.

the other end through the hole in the cardboard. Then thread the string through the hole in the record.

Hold the record by the string and swing it back and forth. Notice that the record keeps tilting in different directions as it swings. Now grab the record. Hold it level and start it spinning. Start swinging the record as it spins. Does the record tilt this time?

The spinning motion keeps the record from tilting. Objects that have a spinning motion resist any force that acts to change their motion.

What Can a Moving Object Do?

You now know that a force can overcome inertia to set an object in motion. Once an object is in motion, you can make it move faster by increasing the force acting on it. If you keep increasing the force, the object will continue to

The harder you pedal, the more force you apply and the faster you make the bike move.

move faster, or **accelerate**. See what you can do when you make an object in motion accelerate.

Making Sounds

You will need:
- helper
- large lid
- pencil
- thick cardboard
- scissors
- pencil
- ruler
- string
- flexible drinking straw

Use the lid to draw a circle on the cardboard. Cut out the circle. Use the pencil to mark nine points spaced evenly around the edge of the circle. Also mark two points on either side of the center of the circle. Poke a tiny hole through all eleven points with the scissors. Then use the pencil to make each hole larger.

Cut a 3-foot (1-meter) length of string. Thread the string through the two holes near the center. Knot the two ends of the string together to make a loop. Bend the straw and place it in your mouth. Ask someone to stretch out the string by placing a finger from each hand through each end of the loop. Next, ask the person to rotate the cardboard circle to twist the string. Then, have the person let go of the circle and pull the string with both hands as soon as the string begins to twist near his or her fingers. As the

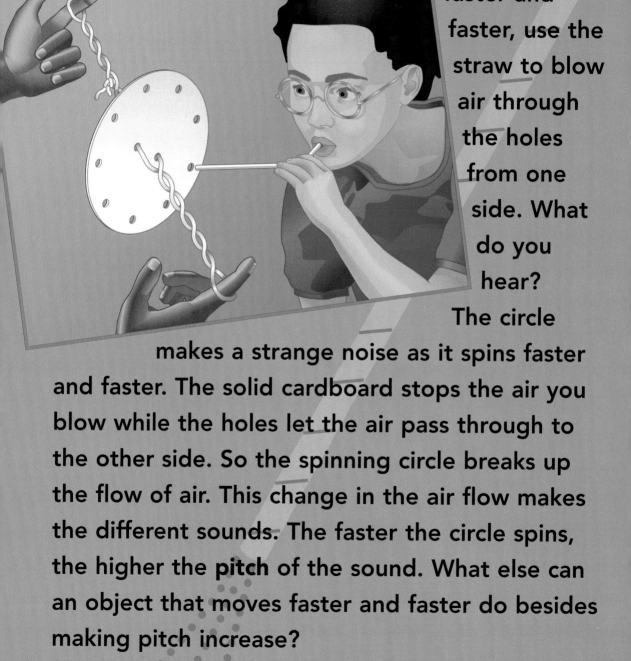

circle spins faster and faster, use the straw to blow air through the holes from one side. What do you hear? The circle makes a strange noise as it spins faster and faster. The solid cardboard stops the air you blow while the holes let the air pass through to the other side. So the spinning circle breaks up the flow of air. This change in the air flow makes the different sounds. The faster the circle spins, the higher the **pitch** of the sound. What else can an object that moves faster and faster do besides making pitch increase?

Lifting It Up

You will need:
- scissors
- empty milk carton (quart size)
- string
- ruler
- wooden spool
- small roll of tape like electrical tape
- marbles

Cut the milk carton in half. Keep the bottom half. Use the scissors to poke a tiny hole on either side of the carton near the top. Cut a piece of string that is about 6 inches (15 cm) long. Tie a knot at one end. Thread the free end through the holes and then tie another knot to make a "handle."

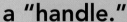

35

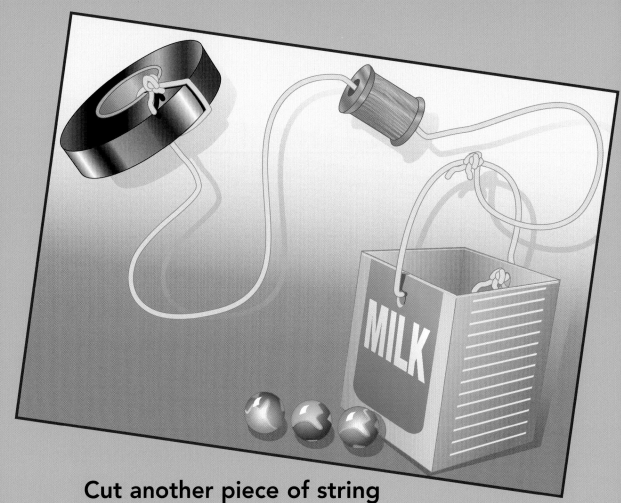

Cut another piece of string
that is about 18 inches (46 cm) long. Tie one
end to the handle. Thread the free end through
a wooden spool. Then tie the free end around a
small roll of tape. Hold the spool in one hand.

Start twirling the spool slowly so that the roll of tape starts spinning around in the air. Slowly make the tape spin faster and faster. What happens to the milk carton?

As the tape spins faster and faster, it provides enough force to lift the milk carton and pull it up toward the spool. How much weight can the spinning tape lift? Experiment by placing marbles inside the milk carton. Add one at a time. How many marbles can the spinning tape lift?

You see motion whenever anything moves. A force is needed to set an object in motion. The force overcomes the object's inertia.

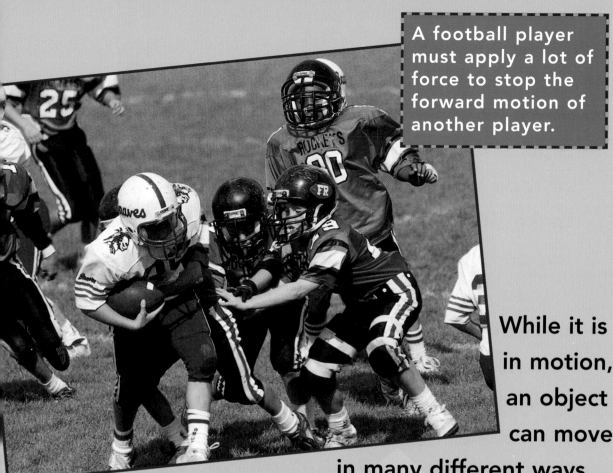

A football player must apply a lot of force to stop the forward motion of another player.

While it is in motion, an object can move in many different ways. If the force on the object keeps increasing, then the object will move faster and faster. A force is also needed to slow down or stop an object in motion. Sometimes, the force has to be very powerful to stop a moving object.

Fun With Motion

Newton actually came up with three laws about motion. His third law states that for every action, there is an equal and opposite reaction. Here is a fun experiment to conduct to see an example of Newton's third law of motion.

Experiment 9

Speeding Along

You will need:
- scissors
- measuring tape
- string
- straw
- balloon
- two helpers
- masking tape

Cut a 10-foot (3 m) long piece of string. Slide the string into the straw. Blow up the balloon. Pinch the opening tightly so that no air escapes. Ask your helpers to use two pieces of masking tape to attach the balloon to the straw. Then have your helpers stretch out the string and hold it tightly and level. Move the balloon and straw toward one end of the string. Release the balloon and watch what happens.

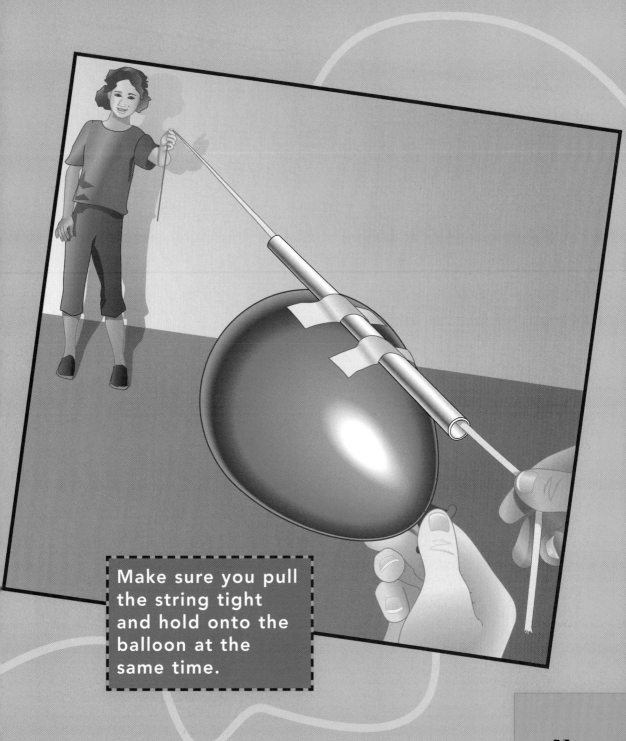

Make sure you pull the string tight and hold onto the balloon at the same time.

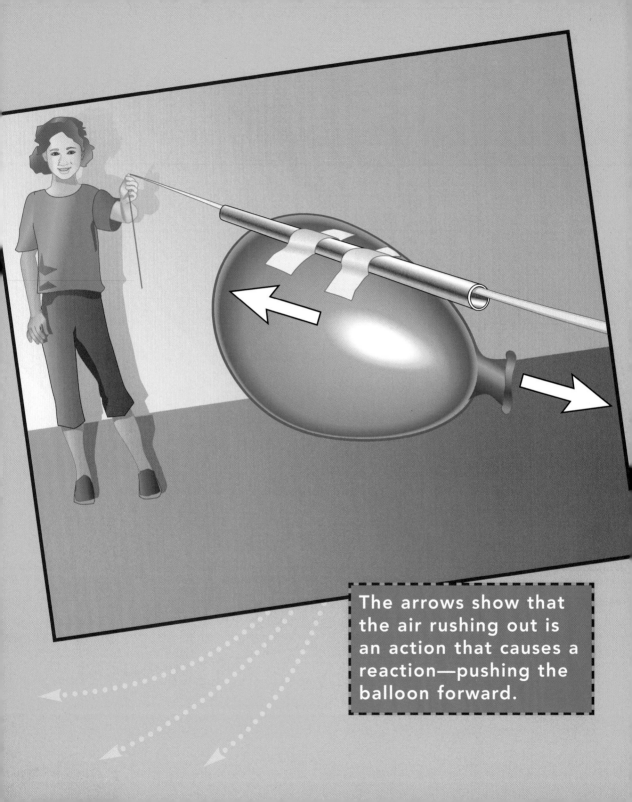

The arrows show that the air rushing out is an action that causes a reaction—pushing the balloon forward.

When you release the balloon, the air inside rushes out the open end. The air rushing out is an action in one direction that causes an equal reaction in the opposite direction. Experiment to test Newton's third law of motion. For example, fill the balloon with only half as much air as you did before. The air rushing out this time should produce an action with only half the force. Does the balloon travel only half the distance this time?

To Find Out More

If you would like to learn more about motion, check out these additional resources.

 **Books**

DiSpezio, Michael. **Awesome Experiments in Force & Motion.** Sterling Publishing, 1998.

Gardner, Robert. **Experiments with Motion.** Enslow, 1995.

Gold-Dworkin, Heidi and Robert K. Ullman. **Learn About the Way Things Move.** McGraw-Hill, 2000.

Graham, John. **Forces and Motion.** Larousse Kingfisher Chambers, 2001.

Madgwick, Wendy. **On the Move.** Raintree Steck Vaughn, 1999.

Murphy, Bryan. **Experiment with Movement.** Lerner Publications, 1992.

Science Museum of Minnesota
120 W. Kellogg Boulevard
St. Paul, MN 55102
651-221-9444
http://www.sci.mus.mn.us/ sln/tf/m/motionmachine/ motionmachine.html

Accept the challenge to use materials left over from a holiday season to make a machine that makes at least one motion. This site will show you some that students submitted, including a dog bone delivery car and an egg cracker.

"Rocket Man"
http://www.discovery cube.org/kids/ rocketMan.htm

This site shows you how to build a simple rocket using plastic film containers. When you blast your rocket into the air, you will see another example of Newton's third law of motion.

"Whirling Watcher"
http://www.exploratorium. edu/snacks/whirling_ watcher.html

Learn how to build a stroboscope that will make a moving object seem to jerk along, change speed, or even move backward.

Important Words

accelerate to increase an object's
  speed

centrifugal force a force on an object
  that keeps it moving around in a
  circle

force the push or pull on an object

inertia the force that makes
  something that is at rest stay still
  and something that is moving stay
  in motion

motion movement

pitch a quality that a sound has

Index

(**Boldface** page numbers
    indicate illustrations.)

acceleration, 31
action, 39, 43
air, 34, 42, 43
backward motion, 23
centrifugal force, 26
changing motion, 29
equal and opposite reaction,
    39, 43
equal force, 14
first law of motion, 10–11
football, **11**, 23, **38**
force, 18–20, 21, 25, 30, 37
    equal, 14
    and forward motion, 38, **42**
    increasing, 30–31
    resisting, 29
force, centrifugal, 26
forward motion, 23, 38, **42**
gyroscope, **29**
inertia, 10–11, 14–15, 17,
    20, 21, 30
    overcoming, 37
laws of motion, 10-11,
    14–15, 39–43
lifting, 35–38
liquids, 16–17, 22
motion, 5, 7, **7**
    changing, 29, 30–31
    fun with, 39–43

kinds of, 23–29
laws of, 10–11, 14–15,
    39–43
stopping, 20, 21–22, 38
what it can do, 30–38
why something moves,
    9–22
motion pictures, 5–8
movie, **4,** 5
Newton, Isaac, 10, 14, 39
object at rest, 10–11
opposite reaction, 39, 43
pitch, 34
pulling, 10, 20
pushing, 10, 20
race horse, 6–8, **7**
reaction, 39, 43
resisting force, 29
resting, 10–11
second law of motion, 14–15
solids, 17, 21
sounds, 32–34
speed, 40–43
spinning motion, 21–22,
    25–26, 34, 37
spiral motion, 23
staying in place, 16–17
stopping motion, 21–22
swinging motion, 24, **24,**
    25–26
third law of motion, 39–43
tilting motion, 27–29

Meet the Author

Salvatore Tocci is a science writer who lives in East Hampton, New York, with his wife, Patti. He was a high school biology and chemistry teacher for almost thirty years. As a teacher, he always encouraged his students to perform experiments to learn about science. He loves to accelerate his convertible sports car to overcome inertia and push it to the speed limit.

Kid Pick!

W9-B-007

Title: _____

Author: _____

Picked by: _____

_____

Why I love this book:

_____

_____

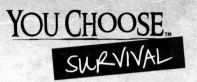

Can You Survive

EXTREME MOUNTAIN
CLIMBING?

An Interactive Survival Adventure

by Matt Doeden

Consultant:
Olivia Sofer
Association of Canadian Mountain Guides Certified Guide
Harvie Heights, Alberta, Canada

CAPSTONE PRESS
a capstone imprint

You Choose Books are published by Capstone Press,
1710 Roe Crest Drive, North Mankato, Minnesota 56003.
www.capstonepub.com

Library of Congress Cataloging-in-Publication Data
Doeden, Matt.
 Can you survive extreme mountain climbing? : an interactive survival adventure /
By Matt Doeden.
    p. cm. — (You choose : survival)
 Includes bibliographical references and index.
 Summary: "Describes the fight for survival while climbing some of the world's tallest
mountains"—Provided by publisher.
 ISBN 978-1-4296-8583-2 (library binding)
 ISBN 978-1-4296-9478-0 (paperback)
 ISBN 978-1-62065-378-4 (eBook PDF)
 1. Mountaineering—Juvenile literature. 2. Survival—Juvenile literature. I. Title.
 GV200.D6393 2013
 796.522—dc23   2012004679

Editorial Credits
Angie Kaelberer, editor; Gene Bentdahl, designer; Wanda Winch, media researcher;
   Danielle Ceminsky, production specialist

Image Credits
Corbis: Aurora Photos/Stefen Chow, cover, Nina Schwendemann, 36, Paul Souders,
16, 22; Courtesy of Kevin Flynn, 80; Courtesy of niyekila 2010, 58, 68; Courtesy of
Olov Isaksson, 46; Courtesy of Wesley Cronk, 27; Dreamstime: Yue Liu, 70; Getty
Images Inc: AFP/STR/Pemba Dorje Sherpa, 97, Aurora/Jake Norton, 85, LOOK/
Bernard van Dierendonck, 62; iStockphotos: Firma Konsultingowa Marek Dziok,
12, ranplett, 32; Shutterstock Maxim Tupikov, 10, Reichtan Sorin, 6, 102, vichie01,
40; SuperStock Inc: imagebroker.net, 90, William Stevenson, 75; © Wolfgang Huber/
MountainSpiritGuides, 43, 49, 53

Printed in the United States of America in Stevens Point, Wisconsin.
122012   007080R

TABLE OF CONTENTS

About Your Adventure.................................... 5

Chapter 1
To the Top! 7

Chapter 2
Conquering Kilimanjaro 13

Chapter 3
Scaling the Matterhorn...........................41

Chapter 4
Everest: The Highest Climb......................71

Chapter 5
To the Extreme.. 103

Real Survivors 106
Survival Quiz 108
Read More 109
Internet Sites 109
Glossary..110
Bibliography..111
Index...112

About Your
ADVENTURE

YOU are a mountain climber about to embark on the adventure of a lifetime. In your quest to reach the top of the mountain, you'll face avalanches, altitude sickness, storms, equipment failure, and more.

In this book you'll deal with extreme survival situations. You'll explore how the knowledge you have and the choices you make can mean the difference between life and death.

Chapter One sets the scene. Then you choose which path to read. Follow the directions at the bottom of each page. The choices you make will change your outcome. After you finish one path, go back and read the others for new perspectives and more adventures.

YOU CHOOSE the path you
take through your adventure.

Mountain climbers get a unique perspective on the world.

To the Top!

Imagine yourself standing on top of one of the tallest mountains in the world. You're looking down at miles of snow, ice, and rock. You're even higher up than the clouds.

The sport of mountain climbing, also known as mountaineering, has been around for thousands of years. The ancient Romans were mountain climbers. So were the Incas of South America and some of the early colonists in North America. But mountain climbing has really taken off in the last 100 years or so.

Turn the page.

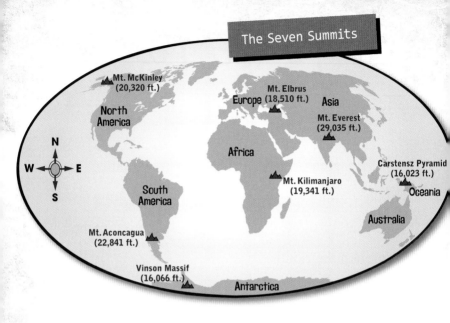

The Seven Summits

Mt. McKinley (20,320 ft.)
North America
Mt. Elbrus (18,510 ft.)
Europe
Asia
Mt. Everest (29,035 ft.)
Africa
Carstensz Pyramid (16,023 ft.)
Oceania
Mt. Kilimanjaro (19,341 ft.)
Australia
South America
Mt. Aconcagua (22,841 ft.)
Vinson Massif (16,066 ft.)
Antarctica

N
W E
S

Modern climbers have reached the top of some of the world's tallest mountains. Some try to climb new, undiscovered routes up famous mountains. Others try for world records. Some make it their life goal to climb the Seven Summits—the highest peaks on each of the seven continents. But most are content to just enjoy the journey and the challenge that mountain climbing provides.

Of course, climbers don't just roll out of bed and head toward a mountain. Their packs are loaded with specialized gear.

Climbers need strong ropes that are dynamic, meaning that the ropes have some stretch. Climbers use specialized knots to attach ropes to harnesses. They also use clips called carabiners to attach ropes to holds placed in the rock. Climbers use belay devices to safely hold a fellow climber. Crampons are metal plates with spikes that attach to boots. The spikes give climbers good footing on snow and ice. Climbers use ice axes to chip into ice sheets.

Even with so much gear, climbing is dangerous. Hundreds of climbers die each year. They freeze in subzero temperatures. They get in the path of avalanches. They die from heart failure and brain hemorrhaging caused by high-altitude illnesses. They fall because of error or equipment failure.

Turn the page.

Belay ropes add a measure of safety to climbs.

Good climbers understand all of these dangers. They know that every time they try to climb a mountain, they are putting their lives at risk. But they keep doing it. They believe the thrill of the climb and the feelings of freedom are worth the risk.

To take a guided climb up Africa's Kilimanjaro, turn to page 13.

To try climbing the challenging Matterhorn, turn to page 41.

To take on the world's highest peak, Mount Everest, turn to page 71.

Zebras graze in the shadow of Mount Kilimanjaro.

CHAPTER 2

Conquering Kilimanjaro

You stare at the great mountain that stands before you. Kilimanjaro looks huge, jutting out above the jungle of Tanzania. It's the highest mountain in Africa at 19,341 feet. You can hardly wait to see the view from the top.

You stand in what's known as the tropical zone. It's the first and lowest point in any ascent of Kilimanjaro. The air is warm and humid, and the grade is shallow. But that will change as you climb.

13

You turn to your guide, Prisca. You and your cousin Mike have hired her to lead you to the top. You're both experienced climbers, but the government of Tanzania only allows guided ascents of the famous mountain.

Turn the page.

"So what will it be?" Prisca asks. You and Mike have narrowed down your choices to two routes. You will either take the Rongai route or the more difficult Shira route.

"We've come all this way," Mike says. "I say go big or go home. Let's try Shira."

"That route is very difficult, even for the most experienced climbers," says Prisca. "There is a good chance we will fail. Rongai is much safer."

They look to you for a decision. Do you want a challenge, or are you more concerned about just getting to the top?

To take the difficult Shira route, go to page **15**.

To take the safer Rongai route, turn to page **18**.

You look at Mike and break out in a big smile. "OK," you say. "Shira it is."

Prisca nods. "OK. We've got a long day ahead of us. We'd better get started."

The three of you travel by truck to the Shira Gate, which is at an altitude of 11,800 feet. Many tourists hire porters to carry their supplies for them, but not your group. You, Mike, and Prisca all carry packs loaded with gear and supplies. You think that carrying your own gear is an important part of the climbing experience.

As you move out of the tropical zone and into the moorland area, you notice that there are few climbers on the trail. There are some easier versions of the Shira route, but it's still not one of the popular routes.

Turn the page.

One of Kilimanjaro's volcanoes formed Lava Tower thousands of years ago.

As you climb, the air grows thinner and cooler. The ground is covered with loose rocks and boulders. You constantly have to watch your footing or risk turning an ankle. You reach camp and stay in tents for the night, but you're back up and moving right away in the morning.

You reach a famous feature on the Shira route—the 300-foot Lava Tower.

"Check it out," says Mike, pointing at a particularly vertical section of volcanic rock. "We've got to climb that."

Prisca says that there's an easier route to the top of the tower. "No need to take chances," she says. But you can see that Mike is determined to go the hard way.

*To find an easier spot, turn to page **20**.*

*To go along with Mike, turn to page **24**.*

"We may never get another chance to do this, Mike," you tell him. "Let's go with Rongai, so we know we'll make it."

"A good choice," says Prisca. "But remember, even Rongai is difficult. There is no guarantee we'll reach the summit."

The three of you begin the ascent. You all carry packs loaded with supplies. It's a five-day journey. Your bodies will need lots of food and water as you work your way up the mountain.

The first few days of your climb are filled with long hikes. The tropical jungle at the foot of the mountain gives way to alpine moorland. Here the air is thinner and cooler. Grasses and shrubs replace the trees. They cling to the rocky ground. Mike complains of headaches, but they're not serious. The three of you are all in great shape.

You continue at a good pace and pass several larger, slower groups along the way. You give a friendly wave and wish your fellow climbers luck in reaching the top. At night you sleep in established camps equipped with huts, tents, and food.

You feel energized on the third day. After several hours of climbing, the three of you arrive at Mawenzi Tarn camp. "This is it for today," Prisca tells you.

"Are you joking?" Mike asks. "We've only climbed a few hours. Let's keep going."

"The next camp is Kibo Hut, and it's at least four hours," Prisca warns you. "It might be best to rest and get used to the altitude here."

They both look at you. What will it be?

*To take it slow and camp here, turn to page **26**.*

*To push on to Kibo Hut, turn to page **28**.*

"Come on, Mike," you tell him. "I know you want to climb, but let's be smart and follow Prisca's lead." Prisca gives you a nod and a small smile.

Mike snorts in disgust but agrees. You follow the established route up the slope, steadily gaining altitude. But once you reach the top of the Lava Tower, you start back down.

"It's important to be moving up and down," Prisca explains. "It helps the body acclimate to the altitude. If you just go straight up, you're much more likely to get altitude sickness."

During the next two days, you realize that she's right. You're already getting headaches. Your appetite is gone, and both you and Mike are feeling dehydrated. You know that you need at least 6 to 8 quarts of water per day. But you have to collect water from mountain streams and then purify it with iodine tablets or chlorine. That's a lot of work.

You've both been skimping on your water, and you're paying the price. Neither of you sleeps well at night. Everything just feels off.

The fifth day is the last part of the ascent. You're that close to the summit. But you feel worse than ever. Your energy is gone.

Prisca encourages you. "Today is the hardest part," she says. "But it's all downhill after that."

The air is so thin up here that you have to stop every few minutes to catch your breath. Mike, who is normally talking every step of the way, barely says a word. He has a crushing migraine headache.

Finally you come over a ridge to Stella Point. You can see the summit from here. But you also notice several guides carrying a man down the mountain. He's suffering from altitude sickness and can't move himself.

Turn the page.

Volcanic rocks cover part of the Shira route.

"I don't think I can do it," Mike says. Every word seems to cause him pain. And you have to agree. The summit, Uhuru Peak, is within sight, but that last climb looks like too much. Prisca tells you that Stella Point is where many climbers quit and turn around. "There's no shame in stopping here," she reminds you.

Mike may be right. If you keep going, you could end up like the man who was being carried down the mountain. Altitude sickness is serious business. Is it worth risking your health to get another few hundred feet higher?

To call it good enough, turn to page 33.

To try to talk Mike into finishing, turn to page 35.

You've come all the way to Africa to climb. You and Mike dig into your packs and pull out your climbing gear. But there are no anchors in the wall, so your ropes, harness, and carabiners won't do you much good.

"That's not very tall," Mike says, pointing at a section of wall about 20 feet high. "We'll just climb bouldering style."

Mike goes first, cramming his hands and feet into small holds and crevices in the rock. He's a natural climber and seems to know just where to find his next hold. Before long, he's reached a flat shelf along the top. "See, piece of cake," he says.

You're next. You grab onto the cool rock and pull yourself up. Prisca waits her turn below. Less than halfway up the rock face, your fingers are burning.

You reach a spot where you need to cross one arm over the other to get the next hold. Mike did it with ease, but your attempt throws off your balance. Your foot slips out of a toehold. For a moment, you are dangling by one hand, 12 feet off the ground. There's no way you can hang on.

You shout as your finger slips, and suddenly you're falling. It's not very far, but the ground below is rocky and jagged. Your ankle turns over badly as you hit the ground, and your hands are cut up as they slam down on a sharp rock.

Prisca rushes up and kneels by your side. "I think your ankle is broken," she says. "We need to get you to a hospital."

Turn to page **37.**

"Let's do this by the book, Mike," you say. He rolls his eyes and shakes his head, but he doesn't argue. You're happy you made the choice. Mawenzi Tarn is absolutely beautiful. You spend the rest of the afternoon exploring and taking in the amazing views near the small mountain lake. You go to bed early, eager to return to the climb tomorrow.

You start out in the morning, filled with energy. But as you get higher and higher, you feel the effects of the altitude. Breathing is a struggle as the air gets thinner. You have to wear more layers to keep warm in the colder air and winds. But your bodies are growing acclimated to the climate. You're able to make good time. You notice several groups turning around.

"They probably climbed too quickly," Prisca says. "That's why it's best to pace yourself." You manage the hike to Kibo Hut without much trouble.

For the final day, you're up early to begin the longest and hardest section of the climb. "This is it," you say to Mike as you strap on your gear.

Mike gives you a playful shove and shouts, "Race you to the top!" He plucks the hat off your head and takes off, charging up the path. He's joking, of course, but you're full of energy and excitement. And of course, you want your hat.

Kibo Hut is the last camp before the summit ascent.

*To chase after Mike, turn to page **30**.*

*To ignore him and save your energy, turn to page **31**.*

You say, "Let's keep going. After all, we're not just tourists. We're climbers. We don't need as much rest as everyone else."

Prisca tries one last time to talk you out of your decision, but you remain firm. With a shrug, she agrees. You stop for a snack and some water, and then keep climbing. Mike seems especially energized. He's almost bouncing up the slope.

But it's not long before neither of you are moving very fast. Your head feels as if it's about to burst. Mike can barely put one foot in front of the other. You stop every few steps to catch your breath.

As Prisca gives you a drink of water, she gives you the bad news. "You're both suffering from altitude sickness. We climbed too high too quickly. Your bodies didn't have enough time to adapt."

"We can't stop now," Mike pleads. "We are so close!"

You wish you could stop and rest a while, but there's no place here to camp. Continuing could be dangerous. And you're not sure you could make it even if you knew it was safe. But Mike looks at you, practically begging you not to call off the climb. The choice is yours.

To turn back, turn to page **33.**

To continue on, turn to page **38.**

"Oh, no you don't!" you shout as you take off after Mike. You know you'll catch him. You're by far the faster runner. But just as you're about to grab him, you step on a large stone. Your ankle turns, and you go sprawling onto the rocky slope.

"Owwwwwwhhhhh!" you shout. Your ankle is throbbing, your hands are scraped to shreds, and your forehead is bleeding.

Mike rushes back to you and shouts for help. "You're OK," he keeps repeating. But you know better. Your ankle is in bad shape.

Turn to page 37.

You roll your eyes and watch Mike horsing around in front of you. You can't blame him for being excited. You are too. But you're going to need your energy for the climb.

A few hours later, Mike isn't laughing anymore. The climbing is hard, and the air is getting thinner with every step. By the time you're scrambling over Gillman's Point, a rocky crater, Mike looks as exhausted as you feel. You're glad you didn't spend your energy goofing around.

"Keep going," Prisca tells you. "This is the hardest part."

You make it up and out of the crater, literally dragging Mike the final few feet. You stop for water and a brief rest before starting the climb again. It's the final stretch.

A few hours later you're pulling yourself up the
final ascent. You raise your arms to the sky as you
reach Uhuru Peak—the highest point in Africa—

and give Mike a hug. You spend only a few minutes
there, taking photos and soaking in the success.
Then it's time to start the journey down. You're
glad that going down is easier than going up.

THE END

To follow another path, turn to page 11.
To read the conclusion, turn to page 103.

You look down and see your hands shaking. Your knees feel ready to buckle out from underneath you. Mike is laboring to breathe, and the pain he's feeling shows on his face. Sadly, you realize that it's just not worth it. You've climbed most of Mount Kilimanjaro. That will have to be good enough.

"OK, let's turn around," you tell Prisca.

You know it's a smart decision, but still, turning around and starting back is hard to do. The summit seems so close, as if you could almost reach out and touch it. But you can't. You've got to think about your health first.

You pull your camera out of your bag, snap a couple of quick photos, and turn back. In your condition, the climb down won't be easy either.

Turn the page.

You know that someday you'll look at those photos with regret. But for now you just want to get down to an altitude where everything doesn't hurt. You're ready for your adventure to end.

THE END

To follow another path, turn to page 11.
To read the conclusion, turn to page 103.

"Come on, Mike," you tell him. "I know it hurts. I'm hurting too. But we've come halfway around the world to get here. We've hiked for five days. Look, there's the peak. We'll never forgive ourselves if we quit now."

Mike manages a slight smile. "Let's do it," he whispers.

You keep going. Every step is agony. About 30 minutes later, you come upon the final section. You have to scramble up the rocky slope. But as you take the final few steps, all your aches and pains seem to fade away.

You and Mike raise your arms and look at each other. "We made it!"

"Congratulations," says Prisca. She gives each of you the Tanzanian Handshake—a celebratory high-five for those who have scaled Africa's tallest mountain.

Turn the page.

As you look out at the amazing view, you know that this is a moment you'll never forget. You can't wait to tell your family about how you conquered Kilimanjaro.

Kibo is one of the mountain's three dormant volcanic cones.

THE END

To follow another path, turn to page 11.
To read the conclusion, turn to page 103.

Prisca calls for help on her radio. There's no way you can walk down the mountain with a broken ankle. Mike sits by your side, waiting for a helicopter to take you to a hospital. "I'm so sorry," you tell him. "You can keep going. I don't mind."

"No, don't worry about it," Mike assures you. "Let's just make sure you're OK."

When the helicopter arrives, medics help you aboard and set your ankle. As the helicopter lifts off, you stare at Kilimanjaro. You can't believe that you came so close without reaching the top.

Mike is right. There will be more mountains to climb and more adventures to take. But you doubt you will ever return to Tanzania. This was your one and only shot to conquer Kilimanjaro, and you couldn't do it. You know you'll always regret it.

THE END

To follow another path, turn to page 11.
To read the conclusion, turn to page 103.

"Let's go," you say, groaning as you struggle to your feet. Prisca tries one last time to talk you into turning around, but you won't listen. Your mind is made up.

The climbing is slower than ever. After an hour has passed, you turn to Mike. His skin looks blue-gray and waxy. "Mike, are you OK?"

He doesn't answer. He barely seems to realize you're there. You grab him by the shoulders, and he collapses. His breathing is low and shallow. Suddenly, he begins to cough. Flecks of blood stain his lips.

"I think Mike's got acute mountain sickness!" you shout. Prisca rushes back. Mike's eyes roll back in his head. He's not responding. His breathing is growing more and more irregular.

Prisca takes a look at Mike. "It's worse than that," she says. "He has high altitude pulmonary edema." That's fluid in the lungs—a very serious medical condition.

Prisca grabs her radio to call in the emergency. But help could be a long time coming, and Mike is slipping into a coma.

"Hang on, Mike!" you whisper in his ear. But you know Mike can't hear you. He's slipping away, and there's nothing you can do. If only you had turned around. No mountain climb is worth losing a friend.

THE END

To follow another path, turn to page 11.
To read the conclusion, turn to page 103.

The Matterhorn stands on the border of Switzerland and Italy.

CHAPTER 3

Scaling the Matterhorn

You feel as if your head is spinning as the cable car sways in the wind. Your Uncle Jack smiles at you. "Don't worry," he says. "Almost everyone who climbs the Matterhorn starts this way."

Of course, you're more worried about the climb ahead than you are about the cable car. You've been practicing for months in climbing gyms and on smaller slopes. You and Uncle Jack even climbed Mount Rainier in Washington to warm up for this trip. But this is the main event.

You've been looking forward to this trip for almost a year. Uncle Jack has been telling you about climbing the Matterhorn since you were a kid. Now you finally get to join him. Are you really ready?

Turn the page.

The Matterhorn is not a simple climb. At 14,691 feet, it's one of the highest peaks in the Alps. It's steep, covered in snow, and completely unforgiving toward those who don't know how to handle it. On average, about 12 people die each year trying to climb it. More than once you've been ready to call off the journey. But now you're here, and you're not about to back out.

The cable car takes you to a point called Schwarzsee. From there, it's a two-hour hike to Hörnli Hut, where you'll stay the night. The hike gives you just a taste of what's to come. You can't take your eyes off the peak. It seems almost impossible that you'll be climbing it tomorrow!

You're glad when you reach Hörnli Hut. You're already more than 10,000 feet above sea level. Staying here will allow your body to acclimate to the thin air and low pressure at this altitude.

Climbers must leave Hörnli Hut before daybreak.

It's early to bed, since your 10-hour climb will start at around 3:30 a.m. Starting then should give you enough time to avoid the thunderstorms that often strike in the evening. Your plan is to climb the east face of the mountain. Jack says that route is better for a less experienced climber like you.

The next thing you know, Jack is shaking you awake. "Are you ready?" Jack asks. "The east face awaits us!"

43

Turn the page.

"Or we could try the north," you say. Jack squints as he looks at you, trying to decide whether you're serious. Truth is, you're not sure yourself.

The east face is no easy climb. But it is well established, with lots of fixed ropes. Because these ropes are already anchored in place, it might be better suited to your level of experience. But you've dreamed of climbing the Matterhorn's north face. It's one of the most challenging and dangerous climbs in the world. You even bragged to some of your friends back home that you were going to climb it. But now that you're here, you don't feel quite as confident.

"Well, it's up to you," Jack says. You know he doesn't think you're ready for the north face. But is he right?

To climb the north face, go to page 45.

To take on the east face, turn to page 48.

You've come all the way to Switzerland to climb the Matterhorn.

"I vote for the north face," you say with a grin.

For a moment, you're afraid Jack will say no. But after a second of hesitation, he smiles, slaps you on the back, and says, "The north face it is."

It doesn't take long before you realize what you've gotten yourself into. Climbing the north face of the Matterhorn isn't for the timid. The slope is steep, and you're constantly on the watch for loose rock. Unlike the more popular east face route, there are few fixed ropes. You and Jack are mostly on your own.

"See that?" Jack asks, pointing ahead. "That's the Traverse of the Angels. This is where the climb gets fun."

Turn the page.

The Traverse of the Angels has seven rock faces.

The traverse is a series of ice-covered rock slabs.
The footing is slick and treacherous. You notice a narrow section that's not covered in ice. "Should we climb there?" you ask, pointing. Even with your trusty ice ax, you feel a lot safer climbing on rock than you do on ice.

"I guess we could try. But you never know if that rock is rotten. It could be dangerous."

You know that rock is rotten when it isn't firmly anchored to the mountain. It's the biggest danger to a climber on the Matterhorn. But climbing on slick ice is no picnic either. There's simply no easy, safe route up the north face.

To continue on ice, turn to page **56**.

To move over to the bare rock, turn to page **64**.

"Maybe the east face would be smarter," you say. You're worried about disappointing your uncle, but he just smiles.

"Good call," he says. "Knowing your limits is a big part of being a good climber. Let's get going. It's going to be a long day."

You soon realize that he's right. On the steep sections, it's one step at a time. Without your crampons and ice ax, you'd have no chance. The going seems slow. But as you and Jack pass a group, you realize that you're making excellent time.

"There's a slab off the main route up ahead," Jack says. "I climbed it with a friend years ago, and it was a lot of fun. What do you say—do you want to take a little detour?"

The route you're on is the one most people use, but it's far from the only way up. There are tons of ways to climb the mountain. You're not forced to stay to a strict path. But on the other hand, the chance of hitting loose rock goes way up if you stray. Is the adventure worth the risk?

© Wolfgang Huber/Mounta InSpiritGuides

The Matterhorn's east face is still a challenging climb.

To take on the slab, turn to page **50**.

To stick to the established route, turn to page **53**.

Jack knows what he's doing. You don't see any reason not to have a little extra fun. "I'm up for it," you say. The two of you veer off the main path, waving happily at the group behind you. After 20 minutes, Jack points ahead. "There it is. Isn't it beautiful?"

You have to admit, it looks like a great piece of rock. It juts up at an angle, but it's rich with handholds and footholds. "There aren't any fixed ropes here," Jack warns. "You've got to be sure of every hold."

Jack starts up. You watch as he grabs, twists, and pulls himself up the slab. You follow behind, mimicking his movements. In one tough section, you have to wedge your entire body between two rocks as you scoot upward to a ledge. But Jack encourages you the whole way, and you have little trouble.

"One last section," Jack shouts down as you grab yet another handhold. You pull yourself up, reach across your body for the next hold, and pull. For a moment, your left hand slips. An image of yourself tumbling down the mountain flashes through your mind. But you hang on, push off on a foothold to lunge up, and pull yourself up and over the final ledge. Whew!

"All right!" Jack says. "Now tell me that wasn't worth a little detour!"

Before long it's back to the main route. You continue up the slope, tracking along a ridge. You scramble up the steep slope and use fixed ropes for the more vertical sections. Your arms and legs are aching. Your head is pounding, probably from the altitude. But Jack keeps pushing you.

Turn the page.

"What do you say about going off course again?" he asks. "I know where there's a fun bit of free climbing."

The last time you veered off course was a blast, but you also had a close call. Now you're even more tired. You're not sure you want to take another risk.

To stick to the fixed ropes, go to page **53.**

To go off course and free climb, turn to page **58.**

Climbers use fixed
ropes to ascend
difficult areas.

You know you're already at the limits of your
skill. "Let's stick to the route," you say.

"Good idea," Jack replies. "Let's stay on task."

You continue up the slope, using a series of
fixed ropes to ascend the most difficult section. You
can't imagine how hard this would be without the
ropes. You're glad you stuck with the plan to climb
the east slope.

Turn the page.

You pass several groups as you climb. Everyone is friendly, and you wish the others luck on their way. Finally you reach the formation known as the Upper Moseley Slab. You're nearing the peak. There are two parties ahead of you, so you wait your turn to climb. You notice that two men are attempting to free climb the slab. "I guess they didn't want to wait," Jack says.

As you're watching them, you see one of the climbers lose his footing. He slips and tumbles about 15 feet down to the ridge below.

You and Jack move to his side as quickly as you can. The man is conscious, but in great pain. He tells you that his name is Vincent. You've taken first aid classes and can see that Vincent is seriously hurt. His left leg appears to be broken, along with his left arm and probably some of his ribs. He may also have a concussion.

As Vincent's friend climbs down, Jack pulls out his satellite phone and calls for help. But you know that help will be slow in arriving. Vincent could go into shock at any moment.

Your first aid training could be a big help in saving Vincent's life. But if you stop here to wait for help, you likely won't have time to complete your ascent. You'll have come all this way without ever reaching the summit.

*To stay with Vincent, turn to page **63**.*

*To continue up the slope, turn to page **68**.*

You take a long look at the bare rock. It looks good, but Jack is right. Best to stay on course. "Let's keep moving," you say.

The footing is slick and scary at times. But you have your crampons and ice ax to keep you steady. Before you know it, you've finished the section. You're breathing heavily from the climb, but you're also pumped up. For the first time, it really feels as if you're going to make it to the top.

After another hour of hard climbing, you stop for a brief rest. Your hands and legs are throbbing. You've got a bit of a headache from the altitude. But despite the pain, you're still smiling, imagining standing at the top of the mountain.

Jack notices your mood. "Don't get ahead of yourself," he warns. "That section is just the start. From here, it starts to get really hard. Check out that section up there."

As you look ahead, you gulp. You're staring at a brutal rock overhang. You've never climbed anything like it. The rock is rough and the holds look good, but you'll literally be dangling over the steep slope as you haul yourself over. You suddenly feel very weak at the knees. You weren't prepared for it to be this hard.

"That's a tough spot for any climber, and it doesn't get any easier after that," Jack says. "The north face is really only for experts. I'm not sure we're up to it. We could always come back later and try an easier route."

You can't argue with him. This section just looks too hard. You don't think you have the skill to take it on. But you've come so far. How can you turn back now?

To turn around, turn to page 66.

To continue, turn to page 67.

57

The Moseley Slabs are located about two-thirds of the way up the Matterhorn.

"Why not?" you answer. "You were right last time."

The Upper Moseley Slab lies ahead. Most climbers use a set of fixed ropes to ascend this part of the mountain. But you and Jack veer off course, avoiding the line of people waiting to use the ropes.

Free-climbing the slab requires your full concentration. In some parts you can scramble up the slope. You carefully watch for rotten rock, which is rock not anchored to the mountain. There are also icy sections that require you to use your ice ax to grip. And then there are the vertical sections, by far the scariest part.

You again follow Jack's lead. You're climbing a vertical section with a small rock overhang. It's one of the most difficult formations to climb, but Jack scales it with no problem.

Just before you hoist yourself over the overhang, one of your hands slips. For a moment, you're dangling by a single hand. You're sure you're going to fall. But Jack grabs your arm before you lose your grip. He helps you up and over onto a flat shelf.

Turn the page.

You plop down, panting. That was way too close to disaster. "I don't know if I can do this, Jack," you admit. "I'm almost out of energy. What if you hadn't caught me?"

Jack nods. "Yeah, that wasn't good. Maybe I'm pushing you too hard. There's no shame in turning around now."

You close your eyes. You'd kind of been hoping Jack would talk you out of turning around. If he agrees with you, maybe you should stop now. But you're so close. Quitting now would be heartbreaking. You try to tell yourself that you can find the strength to keep going.

To get up and keep moving, go to page 61.

To head down the mountain, turn to page 66.

You can't quit now. You know you'll regret it for the rest of your life. You stand up. "I came here to get to the summit, and that's where I'm going."

The two of you continue up the Moseley Slab. It's a tough climb, but you stay focused and clear the slab without any more problems. The next major obstacle is the Shoulder. As you wait to use the fixed ropes, you hear other climbers talking about a man who fell while free climbing the Moseley Slab. You know that could easily have been you.

Finally, it's your turn. Climbing with the fixed ropes seems easy compared to the free climbing you did earlier. Before you know it, you're on the final ascent. It's a steep, rocky section that requires you to climb on all fours.

Just before you reach the summit, Jack stops. "You first," he says. You scramble up to the summit. It feels amazing to be standing at the top of one of the world's most famous mountains.

Turn the page.

The Matterhorn has summits on both the Italian and Swiss sides.

You give Jack a bear hug as he pulls himself up beside you. "We did it," you say. "Best day ever!"

You pull out a little camera and snap a few photos. But then it's time to start back down.

"OK, back to work," Jack says. "You can wipe that grin off your face." But Jack is wrong about that. You doubt you'll stop smiling for a week.

THE END

To follow another path, turn to page 11.
To read the conclusion, turn to page 103.

The other man is Vincent's brother, Anton. They're Italian and speak very little English, but you manage to communicate.

There's no way you can leave Vincent before help arrives. You tell Anton to talk to him, to keep him from losing consciousness. You give Vincent small sips of water and try to keep him warm.

It takes more than an hour for a rescue helicopter to arrive. By the time Vincent is loaded and lifted away, it's too late for you to continue the ascent. But you don't really mind. You could never have felt good about finishing the climb knowing you'd left an injured man behind. Jack doesn't say it, but you know he's proud of you.

The Matterhorn will wait. You fully intend to try climbing it again someday.

THE END

To follow another path, turn to page 11.
To read the conclusion, turn to page 103.

"Let's try it. I always feel safer on rock than on ice," you say. For a moment, it looks as if Jack is going to argue, but instead he just shrugs. "Let's give it a shot."

At first you're glad for your choice. Your footing is much more secure as you work your way up the slope. But as you reach the end of the first long section, a handhold breaks away as Jack is pulling himself up. A rock the size of a football skids past your head, missing you by a few feet. Jack manages to catch himself, and you both get to the top of the section. Your heart is racing.

"Rotten rock," Jack says. "We need to be extra careful here." Your luck isn't as good as you scale the next rock face. Jack is leading the way. You try to mimic all of his handholds and footholds. But in one spot, you have to cross your left arm over your body. It leaves you hanging by one hand for a moment.

You don't feel comfortable with the move, so instead you reach for a higher hold with your left hand. It feels solid. You grab it with both hands and pull yourself up.

It's a huge mistake. You've put all your weight on an unproven hold. The rock gives way under your grasp. Before you realize what's happening, you're falling down the slope. You hear Jack shouting, and you frantically try to grab for something to break your fall. But you've picked up too much speed. Your head smashes against a sharp slab of rock, and you black out. That's for the best. You won't have to feel the rest of the fall that takes your life.

THE END

To follow another path, turn to page 11.
To read the conclusion, turn to page 103.

Every climber must know his or her limits. Those who don't become dead climbers. You thought you were ready to take on this challenge, but now you know you were wrong. It's better to live to climb another day than to push it and take chances that could cost you your life.

"I don't think I can do it," you say, almost in tears. Jack puts a hand on your shoulder. "Don't worry about it. Look how far you came. You made it most of the way up the Matterhorn. How many people can say that? And it's not over. We can always try again."

He's right, but you don't feel consoled. You came to reach the peak, and you failed. It's going to be a long, disappointing descent. Sometimes the right decision doesn't feel very good.

THE END

To follow another path, turn to page 11.
To read the conclusion, turn to page 103.

You know in your heart that this climb is too much for you. But you're not willing to turn around.

You charge ahead with a renewed drive. Jack has to slow you down several times. The overhang looks even tougher from close up. As usual, Jack starts, and you follow. As he swings himself up and over the overhang, his hand slips. In an instant he's falling. Out of instinct, you reach to grab him. As you reach with one hand, your other hand loses its grip.

Suddenly you're falling too. In the final moment before your death, you realize your mistake. The north face of the Matterhorn is dangerous even for the most skilled climbers. You had no business being here. You only wish you'd listened to your gut instinct. But it's too late for that now.

THE END

To follow another path, turn to page 11.
To read the conclusion, turn to page 103.

The other man is Vincent's brother, Anton. The brothers are from Italy and don't speak much English, but you manage to make them understand what they need to know.

"Keep him warm," you tell Anton. You show him that he needs to sit with Vincent, to keep him from slipping out of consciousness. You tell him to give Vincent small sips of water. Then you wish the brothers luck and return on your way.

Climbers approach the Shoulder on their way to the summit.

You and Jack are quiet as you climb the fixed ropes up the Upper Moseley Slab. Your mood is somber as you push up the formation known as the Shoulder. You scramble up the final slope and finally stand atop the Matterhorn.

You raise your arms in the air and shout, but for some reason, your heart just isn't in it. This should be one of the great moments of your life. But all you can think about is Vincent. You wonder whether he's OK.

You can see the same concern in Jack's face. Wordlessly, the two of you nod at each other and begin the long descent. You've succeeded, but somehow, it still feels like failure.

THE END

To follow another path, turn to page 11.
To read the conclusion, turn to page 103.

Mount Everest is in the Himalaya range between Tibet and Nepal.

CHAPTER 4

Everest: The Highest Climb

Your pack is loaded with clothing, lamps, crampons, a climbing harness, an ice ax, and much more. You tie your tightly rolled sleeping bag to the top of your pack and hoist it onto your back.

"Do you think you can lug that thing up to the top of the world and back?" asks Anna, grinning. Anna, Juan, and Peter laugh, and you can't help but join in. The four of you are getting ready to climb the highest mountain in the world. Mount Everest stands 29,035 feet above sea level. Reaching the top is every climber's dream, and you're about to make it a reality.

Turn the page.

You and your three friends have made other big ascents, including Mount McKinley in Denali National Park, Washington's Mount Rainier, and lots of Colorado's highest peaks. But Everest is another thing altogether.

You've got a lot of gear, but your group needs more than you can carry. You'll need tents, food, water purifiers, oxygen tanks, and much more. So you've hired a local guide, Tashi, and several porters to help you scale the mountain. They are local Sherpa people. They're well suited to survive at high altitudes, and they're expert climbers. Only Tashi speaks English, but they all seem friendly and eager to help.

You're almost ready to go. You only have to decide how you're going to climb the mountain.

"I want to take the South Col route," Juan says. "Think about following in the footsteps of Sir Edmund Hillary!"

Anna scowls. She's the youngest of your group and the biggest thrill-seeker. You know that she'll never vote for the easier way. For her, it's not enough to climb the tallest mountain in the world. She wants to do it the hardest way possible. "Who cares about some old guy who climbed Everest 60 years ago? The Northeast Ridge route is more exciting. That's where the hardcore climbing is."

"Doesn't make much difference to me, just as long as we get to the top," says Peter. He turns to you. "What do you think?"

To choose the South Col route, turn to page **74**.

To take on the challenge of the Northeast Ridge route, turn to page **77**.

"I'm with Juan," you say. "Let's do the South Col route. There's no point making things any harder than they already are."

Your long journey begins with a five-day hike to South Base Camp. There's not much hard climbing. This hike is largely about getting your bodies used to working at high altitude. On the first day you're constantly finding yourself short of breath. But by the time you reach the base camp, you feel stronger. After a short stay at the base camp, you're ready to start the real climbing.

Tashi wakes your party up hours before dawn. "We cross the Khumbu Icefall today," he explains. "It's very dangerous. The ice shifts constantly."

You strap on your headlamp and start out. It's bitterly cold. But you make good time. That's critical, because you want to cross the 2,000-foot icefall when it's cold. The warmer it gets, the more dangerous the ice becomes.

Ladders help climbers cross the dangerous Khumbu Icefall.

The icefall is as beautiful as it is terrifying. It's an ever-changing maze of ice blocks, crevasses, and ice ridges called seracs. You hold your breath as you cross huge crevasses on aluminum ladders. In other spots, you have to climb. A fixed rope waits at one large serac, but Tashi goes right past it. It looks as if he wants to lead you around the serac instead of climbing over it.

Turn the page.

"Hey, what's wrong with this spot?" Anna asks. "There's a rope anchored right here."

Tashi shakes his head. "It looks like an old rope. Can't be sure it's strong."

Anna tugs on the rope three times. "Seems strong to me. Let's climb." Peter nods in agreement. Tashi seems unsure. "I'll even go first," Anna says. "I'm the lightest person here."

Climbing here would save a lot of time. The Khumbu Icefall is no place to linger. But is it worth trusting an old rope to save a little time?

To suggest going around the serac, turn to page 79.

To climb the serac, turn to page 93.

"Let's try the north route," you say. "Everybody does the South Col. Let's be different."

The northern route starts in Tibet. You all climb into jeeps for a bumpy ride to Rongbuk Base Camp at the edge of the Rongbuk Glacier. The scenery is breathtaking, although it's hard to enjoy it in the rickety old vehicles. You spend a few days at the camp, taking hikes and getting used to the altitude.

It's time to begin the climb. The first day's journey takes you over a moraine. It's a collection of rocks, from pebbles to boulders, carried down the mountains by glaciers.

"This place is amazing," says Peter, pointing to the huge ice towers that surround you. Juan, who has been fascinated by Everest all his life, explains that the ice towers are the remains of glaciers. "The glaciers carved out this entire valley," he says. "They literally moved mountains."

Turn the page.

The climbing isn't that hard, but even here, you find yourself short of breath because of the altitude. Over the next two days, you trek alongside the glacier. It's a steady climb, with only a few difficult, technical sections. By the end of the second day, you arrive at the wind-blasted Advanced Base Camp (ABC). "This is where the challenge really begins," Juan announces.

Tashi tells you that the next day will be for rest at ABC. The thought of spending a day hanging out here isn't very appealing. "That's crazy," Anna says. "We just started. We do nothing but sit around. There's no reason not to keep going tomorrow."

"Rest and time to acclimate are advised," Tashi insists. Juan nods agreement, but doesn't say anything. Peter looks to you for a decision.

To wait another day, turn to page 84.

To keep going, turn to page 100.

As nice as a shortcut would be, it's just not worth the risk. "It's a bad idea, Anna. Tashi knows what he's doing. Let's follow his lead."

Tashi's route takes a few extra minutes, but you make it out of the icefall with no problems. A valley called the Western Cwm awaits. From here you get your first good look at Everest's summit. It's still 9,000 feet above you. You begin to realize what you've gotten yourself into.

Camp I is at the cwm. You're already exhausted, and you fall asleep as soon as you lay down your head. But early the next morning, Tashi has you on your feet again and ready to go. As your group crosses the Western Cwm, the temperature climbs. You need to shed some layers.

"Where's that famous Everest wind?" asks Peter as he unzips his jacket.

Turn the page.

Climbers cross the Yellow Band on their way to the South Col.

But just minutes later, the wind and cold return. You spend a night at Camp II. The next day you scale the icy blue face of Lhotse, Everest's neighboring mountain. Tashi insists that you all be clipped to a fixed rope as you climb the Lhotse Face and reach Camp III, where you spend the night.

After another day's climbing across the limestone rock of the Yellow Band, you bed down at Camp IV, located at the South Col.

The col is a ridge that separates Everest from Lhotse. Wind rips across the face of the mountain. You rely on bottled oxygen to help you breathe.

Shortly before midnight, you wake up. You and your friends gather to get ready for the day's climb. "We've entered what climbers call the death zone," Juan explains. "We've got two or three days to do this, or we have to turn around."

"Right," Peter says. "We're already at 26,000 feet above sea level. We can only survive here so long, and the clock is now ticking."

Almost on cue, Tashi brings troubling news. Weather reports say that a storm is headed for the area. It doesn't look like a huge one, but climbing during a storm could be deadly. However, waiting here could mean you might never reach the summit.

To climb, turn to page 82.

To wait at Camp IV for better weather, turn to page 95.

"You say it's not a big storm, right?" you ask Tashi.

"Any storm can be dangerous on Everest," Tashi replies. "But you are right. This storm is minor. We could keep going if you are willing to take the risk."

"Then we continue," you say. Anna rushes up to hug you, while Peter and Juan share a high-five. But it's a short-lived celebration. You've got a mountain to climb. Within a few minutes, everyone is all business. You need to reach the summit in the next 12 to 14 hours, or it won't happen.

You make a big push, relying heavily on your oxygen tanks and masks. You reach the area known as the Balcony. It's a rare bit of flat ground on an otherwise steep slope. You rest for a few moments. But as tired as you are, you're eager to get moving. The wind is howling and snowflakes are flying.

"We're … almost … there," Peter shouts into the wind, taking a breath between every word. You don't bother to speak at all. A thumbs-up is all the energy you care to spend on conversation.

You continue to move up the ridge, but the steep slopes force you onto areas covered by deep snow. Tashi selects your route carefully. You seem to be moving at a crawl.

Anna turns to you. "We need to move faster."

It's true. At this pace, it seems as if you'll never make it in time. But Tashi has done this so many times before—you should probably trust his lead.

To let Tashi set the pace, turn to page **97**.

To ask Tashi to speed up, turn to page **99**.

"Everest isn't going anywhere," you say with a sigh. "We can wait another day."

Later you're glad that you did wait. You and your friends all have headaches from the altitude. The rest gives you each a chance to catch up on much-needed sleep. By the next day your headache is all but gone, and you're ready to go.

The day's climb takes you onto the Rongbuk Glacier. You all put on your crampons for the trek over the huge ice sheet. Lots of fixed ropes help you climb the near-vertical sections here.

You reach the North Col, a valley that separates Everest from nearby Changtse. From there, it's on to Camp V. You rely more on the oxygen tanks your porters are helping carry up the mountain.

"If breathing is this hard at 25,000 feet, I can't even imagine what it'll be like at the summit," Peter says. "I'm not sure I'll be able to do it."

Most climbers need extra oxygen at the death zone and above.

"A lot of people can't," Juan replies. He's right. Most attempts to climb Everest end in failure.

After a day's rest at Camp V, it's time for the final push. "This is it," Juan says. "Once we leave camp, we enter the death zone. That's what they call anything above 26,000 feet. The human body just can't survive it for more than a couple of days. We'll have two or three days, tops, to get to the summit. Otherwise, we have to turn back."

Turn the page.

As you climb, you understand the term "death zone." The air up here is so thin that you have your oxygen mask on almost all the time.

After about five hours, you reach Camp VI. It's at 27,000 feet, and the view is spectacular. But there's a problem. Tashi tells you that a small storm is on its way. Climbing tomorrow might be too dangerous. He suggests waiting here an extra day.

"No chance!" Anna says. "We're so close. If we only have two or three days, we can't afford to spend one sitting here."

Peter nods. You can tell that Juan is struggling with the decision. He knows the danger of climbing in bad weather but can't bear the thought of failing to reach the top.

To take your chances and continue, go to page 87.

To wait an extra day here, turn to page 95.

"Tashi, you said it's a small storm, right?"
The guide nods. "OK then, let's keep going. If it
gets too bad, we'll turn around."

Anna gives you a hug, Peter slaps a high-five,
and Juan breathes a sigh of relief. Nobody wants to
turn around when you're this close.

The wind howls and snow falls, but as storms
here go, it's pretty minor. But it does make the
climb more difficult. You make your way into a
treacherous section called the Yellow Band. This
near-vertical climb features lots of fixed ropes, but
Tashi warns you to choose carefully. "Many of
these ropes are old," he says.

You find out what he means when Juan clips
into one and tugs. The rope snaps in half, coiling
down the steep slope. Juan's eyes are huge. "Aren't
you glad you gave it a good tug first?" Anna asks.

Turn the page.

You work your way up the Yellow Band and over a limestone ledge called the First Step. The Second Step is harder still. You use a 30-foot aluminum ladder placed by climbers in 1975.

"I can't believe I'm climbing up Everest on a ladder!" Peter says. You're too short of breath to bother laughing. In fact, you're having trouble breathing at all. Your headache is back, fiercer than ever. You're even finding it hard to walk in a straight line at times.

From the Second Step, it's on to the Third Step. "There are two ways to go here," Tashi explains. "We can go around and climb up the loose rock, or tackle it head on, straight up."

"Head on!" Anna says.

"I say let's go around," Peter says. "It's safer."

To go with the safer route, go to page **89.**

To tackle the Third Step head on, turn to page **91.**

You just roll your eyes. "As if being near the top of the world's tallest mountain isn't enough adventure! Let's be smart. Tashi, lead the way."

You skirt around the rock face, scrambling up broken rocks and gullies. As you pull yourselves up that final step, all that remains is the summit. This final rock face is steep and snow-covered.

Your first instinct is to hurry, but quickly you realize that you have to take your time. Slowly, carefully, you work your way up. One by one, you track along a narrow ridge. The wind howls, making you aware of the fall if you should lose your footing. But your steps are surefooted and steady.

Juan is the first to the summit. Anna follows, and then you and Peter. You peel off your oxygen masks and shout down at the world below.

Turn the page.

Buddhist prayer flags decorate Mount Everest's summit.

"We did it!" Juan screams at the top of his lungs. Anna is doing a little dance. Peter is on one knee. You're not sure, but you think he might be crying. You look out below you. This is as high up as anyone on the planet can stand. You are literally on top of the world. It's a sight and a moment you will never forget.

THE END

To follow another path, turn to page 11.
To read the conclusion, turn to page 103.

You look at the rock face ahead of you, asking yourself whether you can do it. "No way," Juan says. "Let's be smart here," Peter adds. Anna just looks at you, desperate to climb this dangerous rock face. You realize that you agree with her. You came for adventure. Why not go the hard way?

"Peter, Juan, you guys go with Tashi. We're going to have some fun."

And it is fun. You climb the step along a series of ledges. You have to be extra careful. Anna goes first and then belays for you. She extends enough rope for you to climb and then applies friction with a belay device to keep you from falling.

You stop and rest on a ledge, panting heavily. "Next!" Anna says, eager to keep going.

"Right behind you. Give me a second."

Turn the page.

But before you can stand up, disaster strikes. Anna reaches for what looks like a simple handhold, but it crumbles under her grasp. She loses her balance and teeters off the edge of the ledge. Instinctively, you reach out to save her. But your momentum does more harm than good. Just then a huge gust of wind whips around the mountain. It's all too much. You both lose your grasp. Your rope breaks free from its anchor, and you're falling over the ledge.

In a moment, your world is a confused jumble of falling, smashing into rocks and ice, and falling again. Lucky for you, it's not long before you're knocked unconscious. You know you won't be waking up again. You took one too many chances, and now you're paying the price.

THE END

To follow another path, turn to page 11.
To read the conclusion, turn to page 103.

What fun is going the slow way? "I'm with Anna," you say.

Tashi tries once again to talk you out of using the rope, but Anna is already clipping herself in, locking her harness to the fixed rope with a bright red carabiner. You stand below and secure the other end of the rope to your belay device. It allows you to feed her slack in the rope as she climbs, but catch her if she slips. You suggest handholds and footholds as she scales the rock.

Anna is two-thirds of the way up the serac when Peter shouts out. "The rope is coming apart!"

He's right. Near the top of the serac, where the rope is anchored, the strands of rope are giving way. Everything happens in a flash. The weakened rope snaps. Anna is trying to grab for a new handhold. In a moment, she's lost her grip and is falling. She lands on her back with a terrible thud.

Turn the page.

Juan rushes to Anna's side, with you and Peter only a few steps behind. She's unconscious and not breathing. Blood is gushing from a wound on her head, and it looks as if at least one arm is broken. "Call for help!" you shout to Tashi.

But deep down, you know it's too late. Anna isn't going to make it. Your attempt to climb Everest is a failure, and you're about to lose one of your best friends. You silently curse yourself for letting her take such a reckless risk. Everest is dangerous enough on its own.

THE END

To follow another path, turn to page 11.
To read the conclusion, turn to page 103.

Climbing Everest is difficult and dangerous under the best of conditions. You're not eager to try it during a storm.

"We'll wait," you tell Tashi. You hear Anna and Peter both groan at the thought of waiting. Even the usually careful Juan looks disappointed.

Several hours later, the storm rolls through. The wind picks up a little, and snow falls, but it's really not much of a storm. But by the time it's over, it's too late to start climbing for the day. That means another night spent at camp.

More bad weather comes the following day. As you peer out of your tent, watching the swirling snow, you know your chance to climb Everest is slipping away.

"It's over," Juan says with a sigh. "We'll never make the summit now."

Turn the page.

"But we have oxygen," Anna says. "We can still do it."

Peter puts a hand on her shoulder. "Juan is right. I've already got splitting headaches. I'm not sure I'd want to continue even if it was safe. And Tashi says it's time to start heading back down. Face it, it's over."

Nobody says anything directly, but you can tell that all three of your friends are angry and disappointed. They don't say much to you. You know they resent the decision that you made to stop the climb. You've cost them their chance at Everest. You can only hope they'll forgive you.

THE END

To follow another path, turn to page 11.
To read the conclusion, turn to page 103.

"Relax," you say. "Tashi's testing every step to make sure he doesn't set off an avalanche. Do you want to be buried under 100 tons of snow?"

Even Anna doesn't have an argument for that. So you continue moving at a slow pace until you've got solid ground underneath you again.

You're getting closer. You have to climb some of the most treacherous patches of rock and ice before finally reaching Hillary Step. The 40-foot rock wall is the last obstacle between you and the summit.

Hillary Step is named for Sir Edmund Hillary.

Turn the page.

You watch each of your friends make that final climb on fixed ropes. Then it's your turn. You tap strength you didn't even know you had as you scale that final wall. From there it's a relatively easy scramble to the peak. The four of you stand there together, hugging, high-fiving, and even shedding a few tears. The view is breathtaking from the top of the world. It's a moment you know you will never forget.

THE END

To follow another path, turn to page 11.
To read the conclusion, turn to page 103.

You and Anna move a little faster to walk alongside Tashi. "We're never going to make it at this speed," Anna says. "We need to go faster."

Tashi shakes his head, but you chime in. "Just a little faster, Tashi. We're so close."

The guide slumps his shoulders and picks up the pace. But just then a single footstep sets off disaster. It starts with a small clump of snow breaking free underfoot. Then more snow follows. Within moments, you're staring at an avalanche. Everything happens so fast, there's almost nothing you can do. You see Peter swept away down the slope before your own footing gives way.

You're lucky. You slam your head against a rock. That saves you the terror of being awake as you suffocate under thousands of pounds of snow.

THE END

To follow another path, turn to page 11.
To read the conclusion, turn to page 103.

"Anna's right," you say. "We didn't come half way around the world to sit in tents. Let's go!"

Tashi shrugs. "All right, then. Get your gear together and let's start."

That morning as you climb onto the Rongbuk Glacier, you're glad you decided to move. It's a beautiful day. You attach crampons to your boots for better traction. You're making excellent time. Tashi urges you to pace yourselves, but you're too excited to take it slow.

You reach the North Col. "It's time to climb!" Anna shouts. She's right. Fixed ropes await you, and the four of you eagerly clip in and start up the rock face. You try to ignore a growing headache as you near the top. Within only a few hours, you've conquered the col and reached the next camp.

"See," Anna brags. "We didn't need to rest."

But that night, you feel weak. Your headache grows worse, until all you can do is bury your face in your sleeping bag. You know that the others are experiencing similar problems. Peter has vomited several times, and nobody wants to eat. Even Tashi looks sick.

By morning you can't even think of climbing. Everything hurts. When Juan begins coughing up blood, you know you've made a critical mistake.

"We must descend," Tashi says. "Get your gear. We leave now."

This time, you don't argue. All you want is to get down to an altitude where you can breathe. You've learned a valuable and expensive lesson. To climb Everest, you need to take your time. If you ever make it back here, you'll know better.

THE END

To follow another path, turn to page 11.
To read the conclusion, turn to page 103.

Smart climbers get in top shape before attempting a climb.

CHAPTER 5

To the Extreme

Extreme mountain climbing is serious business. Many climbers believe that nothing can top the feeling of reaching a mountain summit. But it's a long, difficult journey. And if you've never climbed before, how can you know whether you have what it takes?

What do you do if you're really interested in becoming a climber? You've already taken an important first step by reading about the sport. Keep it up! Read books and magazines about climbing. Check out Internet sites devoted to the sport. And if you're serious, start training.

If you live in or near a large city, the odds are good that there's a rock climbing gym in your area. Gyms are a great place to get a start in the sport.

Experts at gyms can introduce you to the basics. You can practice climbing in a safe environment, learn about climbing gear, and master techniques such as belaying. It's a good idea to also learn first aid so you can help yourself or a fellow climber.

Once you've got the basics down, it's time to head outside. But don't go straight for one of the Seven Summits! Find small climbs suited for beginners. Build up your strength and stamina. If you can, train at high altitude. Oxygen levels and air pressure decrease at high altitudes. Your body needs time to adapt.

It's easy to get carried away in the excitement of a climb. But remember that good climbers always put safety first. They care for their equipment and inspect it before every climb. They know their limits. If a climb is too hard, or the weather is too bad, they know to turn around. Live to climb another day!

And remember, only experts should ever climb alone. You can hire a certified mountain guide to help you on a climb, especially when you're a beginner. To find a certified guide, you can contact an organization such as the American Mountain Guides Association or the Association of Canadian Mountain Guides.

Climbing can be a lot of fun. But always remember that it's dangerous. Take responsibility for yourself and your own safety. Don't count on others to bail you out if you get in over your head. If you're safe and smart, you'll have a lifetime of climbing adventures ahead of you.

REAL SURVIVORS

Joe Simpson and Simon Yates

In 1985 mountaineers Joe Simpson and Simon Yates set out to climb Siula Grande in the Andes Mountains of Peru. Simpson and Yates were connected by a rope when Simpson broke his leg and slipped over a cliff. For an hour, Yates tried to hold on, but Simpson's weight was too much. He had no choice but to cut the rope and let his friend fall. Yates assumed Simpson was dead and went back down alone. But Simpson survived. Over the next three days, Simpson pulled himself down the mountain, despite agonizing pain. Simpson said later he would have done the same thing as Yates had he been in the same position.

Colby Coombs

In 1992 Colby Coombs was climbing with his friends Tom Walter and Ritt Kellogg. The trio was about 4,000 feet from the top of Mount Foraker in the Alaskan range. They were tied together when an avalanche struck. Coombs lost consciousness as he fell 1,000 feet down the mountain. Six hours later, he awoke. He was hanging in the air, still attached to the rope. His friends were dead. Coombs had several broken bones, including two in his neck. For five days he endured incredible pain to climb down the mountain. When he reached base camp, he had to wait four days for weather to clear enough for a plane to take him to a hospital.

Jon Krakauer

In 1996 writer Jon Krakauer joined an Everest expedition to research a story. Krakauer's group joined with two other climbing groups. When the group was at the summit, bad weather rolled in. Before long the group was trying to descend in a blizzard. One guide and one fellow climber died near the summit, probably from a fall. Several climbers were lost as they tried to make their way down. The blizzard lifted the next day, and what remained of the group was able to descend. In all, eight people died on the mountain that day. Krakauer wrote the best-selling book *Into Thin Air* about the ordeal.

Adam Potter

In 2011 Adam Potter was climbing Scotland's Sgurr Choinnich Mor. As he hiked along an icy patch near the summit, he lost his footing. Potter fell more than 1,000 feet. When he regained consciousness, he stood up, despite a broken back. He looked at a map to figure out where he was. A rescue helicopter flew past him. The crew didn't believe that the man standing in the snow could be the victim! The crew picked up Potter later, after his friends identified him.

SURVIVAL QUIZ

1. Which device would be helpful if you need better footing while climbing on a glacier?
A. A carabiner
B. A harness
C. Crampons
D. A belay device

2. Altitudes 26,000 feet and higher are known to climbers by what name?
A. The summit
B. The death zone
C. Cols
D. The stratosphere

3. Which of the following is a major danger to climbers?
A. Equipment failure
B. Avalanches
C. Bad weather
D. All of the above

4. Which of the following is not a symptom of altitude sickness?
A. Sneezing
B. Headache
C. Confusion
D. Shortness of breath

Answers: C, B, D, A

Read More

Brown, Alex. *Mountain Adventures.*
Mankato, Minn.: Smart Apple Media, 2009.

Hurley, Michael. *The World's Most Amazing Mountains.* Chicago: Raintree, 2009.

Piper, Ross. *Death Zone: Can Humans Survive at 26,000 Feet?* Mankato, Minn.: Capstone Press, 2008.

Shone, Rob. *Defying Death in the Mountains.*
New York: Rosen Central, 2010.

Internet Sites

Use FactHound to find Internet sites related to this book. All of the sites on FactHound have been researched by our staff.

Here's all you do:
Visit *www.facthound.com*
Type in this code: 9781429685832

Glossary

acclimate (AK-luh-mayte)—to get used to something

altitude (AL-ti-tood)—height above sea level

avalanche (AV-uh-lanche)—a mass of snow, rocks, ice, or soil that suddenly slides down a mountain slope

belay (bih-LEY)—the act of applying friction to a rope so that another climber does not fall

bouldering (BOHL-duhr-ing)—a type of free climbing in which no ropes are used

carabiner (kar-uh-BEE-nuhr)—a metal clip that climbers use to attach themselves to climbing ropes

col (KOL)—a valley or depression between mountains

crampon (KRAM-pahn)—a spiked iron plate attached to a climber's boot to give better footing

cwm (COOM)—a valley

moorland (MOOR-land)—an area of dry, open wasteland, common at high altitudes

serac (suh-RAK)—a steep ice formation in a glacier

traverse (truh-VURS)—a crossing

BIBLIOGRAPHY

Connally, Craig. *The Mountaineering Handbook: Modern Tools and Techniques That Will Take You to the Top.* Camden, Maine: Ragged Mountain Press, 2005.

Cooke, Carlton, Dave Bunting, and John O'Hara, eds. *Mountaineering: Training and Preparation.* Champaign, Ill.: Human Kinetics, 2010.

Eng, Ronald C., ed. *Mountaineering: The Freedom of the Hills.* Seattle: Mountaineers Books, 2010.

Messner, Reinhold. *Everest: Expedition to the Ultimate.* Seattle: Mountaineers, 1999.

Royal Geographical Society. *Everest: Summit of Achievement.* New York: Simon & Schuster, 2003.

Stewart, Alex. *Kilimanjaro: A Complete Trekker's Guide.* Milnthorpe, U.K.: Cicerone, 2011.

INDEX

acclimation, 19, 20, 26, 42, 74, 77, 78, 84, 104

avalanches, 9, 97, 99, 106

bouldering, 24

Coombs, Colby, 106–107

equipment
  belay devices, 9, 10, 91, 93, 104
  carabiners, 9, 24, 93
  climbing ropes, 9, 10, 24, 91, 92, 106
  crampons, 9, 48, 56, 71, 84, 100
  fixed ropes, 44, 45, 50, 51, 53, 58, 61, 69, 75, 76, 80, 84, 87, 93, 98, 100
  harnesses, 9, 24, 71, 93
  ice axes, 9, 46, 48, 56, 59, 71

Everest, Mount
  camps, 74, 77, 78, 79, 80, 84, 85, 86, 95, 100
  Hillary, Sir Edmund, 72, 73, 97
  Khumbu Icefall, 74–75, 76, 79
  Lhotse Face, 80, 81
  North Col, 84, 100
  Northeast Ridge route, 73, 77–78, 84–91, 95–96, 100–101
  Rongbuk Glacier, 77, 84, 100
  seracs, 75, 93
  South Col route, 72, 73, 74–76, 77, 79–83, 95–99
  Yellow Band, 80, 87, 88

illnesses
  acute mountain sickness, 38
  altitude sickness, 9, 21, 20, 23, 28, 101
  high altitude pulmonary edema, 39

Kilimanjaro, Mount
  Kibo Hut, 19, 26, 27
  Lava Tower, 16, 17, 20
  Mawenzi Tarn, 19, 26
  Rongai route, 14, 18–19, 26–34, 38–39
  Shira route, 14, 15–17, 20–25, 33–36, 37
  Stella Point, 21, 22
  Uhuru Peak, 22, 32
Krakauer, Jon, 107

Matterhorn
  east face route, 43, 44, 45, 48–55, 58–63, 68–69
  Hörnli Hut, 42, 43
  Moseley Slabs, 54, 58, 61, 69
  north face route, 44–47, 56–57, 64–67
  Shoulder, 61, 68, 69
  Traverse of the Angels, 45, 46

oxygen, 72, 81, 82, 84, 85, 86, 89, 96, 104

Potter, Adam, 107

rotten rock, 46–47, 59, 64

Seven Summits, 8, 104
Simpson, Joe, 106

training, 41, 103, 104

water, 18, 20–21, 28, 31, 63, 68, 72

Yates, Simon, 106